TALKING ABOUT

Being an Immigrant

Sarah Levete

Franklin Watts
London • Sydney

© Aladdin Books Ltd 2005

Designed and produced by
Aladdin Books Ltd
2/3 Fitzroy Mews
London W1T 6DF

First published in
Great Britain in 2005 by
Franklin Watts
96 Leonard Street
London EC2A 4XD

ISBN: 0 7496 6255 7

Design: PBD; Flick, Book
Design and Graphics

Picture research:
Pete Bennett & Rebecca Pash

Editor:
Rebecca Pash

The consultant, Don Flynn,
is Policy Officer for the Joint
Council for the Welfare of
Immigrants.

501342163

Contents

"Who are immigrants?"

People often travel from one country to another. It may be to go on holiday or visit relatives, but they usually return home after a week or two. Sometimes, people travel to another country and stay there. People who move permanently to another country are called immigrants.

A person who moves permanently to another country is an immigrant.

Look around you at school or in the street. Any one of the people you see may be an immigrant. Immigrants can be young or old, and can come from any country or background. Perhaps someone from another country has moved into your street or started at your school. Maybe you or one of your parents used to live in a different country. This book explains what it is like to move to a new country and discusses the issues and feelings involved.

"What does the word 'immigrant' mean?"

For centuries, people have travelled across the world to settle in other countries. This is known as "migration". To "emigrate" means to leave one's own country to move to another. To "immigrate" means to come to another country to live. An "immigrant" is someone who has moved into a new country to settle there.

The U.S.A. is often called a country of immigrants. People from all over the world have settled there.

Some of the first immigrants fled danger or poverty to find a better life elsewhere. Later, others sought wealth and opportunity in newly discovered countries such as the United States of America and Australia.

Today, there are no new countries to discover! But people still emigrate all over the world. People with different skin colours, who belong to different religions, speak different languages and have different ways of life, called cultures, live side by side. We say these communities are "multicultural".

Did you know...

Aborigines lived in Australia long before the first immigrants settled there. Aborigines are the "native" or "indigenous" people of Australia. The first immigrants who settled in the country were also known as "colonists". They took control of Australia, enforcing their rules and ways of life without respecting those of the Aborigines.

"Why do people want to live in another country?"

People decide to live in a new country for many different reasons. It may be because of a job offer in another country. Some people want to live in a hot country, and decide to move somewhere sunny such as Australia or Spain. If a person's partner or relatives live in a different country, he or she may emigrate to that country. Others go to countries where they can earn more money.

A family may settle in another country if a parent has a new job there.

Many people emigrate because of more serious and dangerous concerns. Some are forced to leave their own country because of war and fear for their safety. If there is a lack of food, water or medicine, a person may decide to try and find a better quality of life in another country.

My story

"My dad was offered a job in Australia. We all moved here a year ago. Now we're here, I really like it. But it's taken quite a long time to get used to it."
Barnaby

"What is it like to leave your home?"

Emigrating means saying goodbye to friends and family, and everything that feels familiar. You may feel very anxious about what life will be like in another country. It can be overwhelming at first, but new experiences often turn out to be fun!

For many people, emigrating is an exciting new start. It is a chance to see and do new things and to meet new people.

You can stay in contact with friends and family, and share your new experiences with them.

Sometimes, in countries where there may be fighting or a war, people often have to leave their homes with little warning because they are in danger. They may have to leave their family and belongings behind without knowing where they are going and whether they will ever be able to return.

Think about it

Imagine what it is like to leave your home with no time to pack or say goodbye to friends and family. You might not know where you are going, how your journey will be made or what will happen when you arrive. People in this situation have to cope with great fear, danger and uncertainty. Arriving in a different country where they might not speak the language can be equally as frightening.

"Where is there to go?"

Over the past sixty years, it has become easier to travel across the world, and more and more people have emigrated. In response to the increasing number of immigrants, many countries have introduced rules stating who can and can't live in their country. These immigration rules affect a person's choices about where to emigrate.

Countries often welcome skilled workers from other countries.

People with special skills, such as doctors, are welcomed by many countries. However, there is also a great need for people to work in less skilled jobs such as cleaning or brick laying. The immigration rules for these workers are often more difficult and they may be refused entry by some countries.

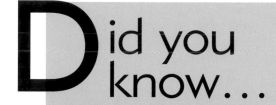

Did you know...

Immigration laws can make it difficult for unskilled people to find a new home. To avoid the restrictions, some people enter a country illegally, putting themselves at great risk. They may hide for days in lorries or aeroplanes, or travel on overcrowded, unsafe boats.

"What happens when you arrive?"

To enter a country, a person needs the correct documents. These include a passport and, in some cases, a visa that confirms the person has the right to enter the country.

People without the correct documents face difficulties. They may be refused entry and sent back to the country they came from. Or they may face a wait while officials decide if they can stay.

Some people may have to prove that it is unsafe to return to their own country.

A person who flees his or her country because of fear and danger is called a refugee. If he or she seeks safety, or "asylum", in another country, he or she is known as an asylum seeker. Each person has a human right to seek protection in another country. Government organisations consider each individual's circumstances and decide whether or not a person can stay in the country.

Did you know...

Everyone should be able to live in his or her own country without fear or danger. But many people are threatened or attacked because of their religious or political beliefs. This is known as "persecution". Some leave their country in desperation and seek safety or asylum elsewhere.

"How does it feel to be an immigrant?"

Some people feel welcomed and happy as they arrive in another country. They may have relatives to help them, a job to start or enough money to find a home.

For those who have fled their country there is great uncertainty. Many have to wait for a decision on whether or not they can stay. They may have to fill in difficult forms or pay fees to get the right papers. This experience can be very worrying.

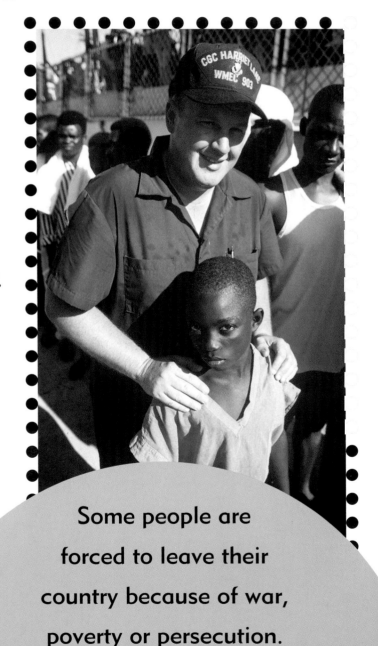

Some people are forced to leave their country because of war, poverty or persecution.

Whatever the reason for emigrating, most people will have left behind friends and family. Even if a person is moving to a new job and home, he or she may be anxious about fitting in and adjusting to different ways of doing things.

Everything may be new – from the weather to where you go to school. It's not easy to get used to the way the trains and buses work, to find places to shop, or to work out the currency used. You may even have to learn a new language.

My story

"When we arrived, I was really excited. But everything is so different. Mum and Dad are out at work all day and it's quite hard getting used to a new school. I miss my old friends but I've got a photo album to remind me of them. Hopefully, I'll soon be able to put photos of new friends in it."
Oscar

"How do I fit in?"

Your new school may seem strange at first, especially if you don't speak the language. It can take time to make friends and feel settled. Taking part in activities you enjoy, and trying some new ones can help you feel as if you belong. It's also hard for grown-ups to feel at home in a new country. They may find it hard to get a job or meet other people. They can feel quite isolated and lonely, so try to be understanding.

At first you may feel you will never fit in, but in time you will feel more settled.

If someone from another country has recently arrived in your area or school, make a special effort to help him or her feel welcome. You could invite them to join in with your activities or offer your help. You may not understand each other's language, but you can show kindness without words.

Think about it

When a young person moves to a new country, he or she may be influenced by the way other young people behave. This can cause conflict at home. Try to consider your parents' viewpoint and don't let others put pressure on you. Discuss your feelings with your family and see if you can agree on what is and isn't OK.

"Where do I belong?"

When you arrive in another country, you may feel unsure about where you belong. Your new home will probably be very different from your old home – it may not feel like home at all. But remember you can be a part of both countries and cultures.

You may meet or live near people who share the same country of birth, religion or culture as you. This can make it easier to feel at home, but it can also make it difficult to get to know other local people.

Many immigrants feel part of both the country they have moved to and the country in which they were born.

It helps to understand and respect any differences between your culture and the culture of your new country. In return, people should accept you for who you are and respect your beliefs and culture.

Did you know...

After living in a country for a certain length of time, immigrants can apply to be a "citizen" of that country. Citizenship gives people rights, such as the right to vote in that country's elections. Many citizens of a country can trace their family history back to find people who arrived as immigrants.

SALZBURG
HAUPTBAHNHOF

"Will people treat me differently?"

You have every right to live in your new country. Whatever your reasons for moving, you should be treated with respect and made to feel welcome.

Unfortunately, some people treat immigrants unfairly and unkindly. Treating someone badly because he or she is from a different country or culture, or because they have a different skin colour, is called "racism".

It is wrong to treat a person differently because he or she comes from another country.

Racism is any form of action that is intended to hurt, offend or disadvantage someone because of their skin colour, culture or religion – their "race". Racism is not OK, and should not be ignored. If you experience racist bullying, or see it happening, tell a teacher or another grown-up you trust. This kind of behaviour is not acceptable.

My story

"My dad is a doctor where we come from. But because he doesn't have the right papers, he can only work packing boxes here. Some people say mean things about me and my family, but I know that we all work hard and have every right to be here. I ignore mean comments and choose friends who like me just as I am."
Jacob

"Why are some people against immigration?"

Some people are afraid of things that are new to them. If large numbers of immigrants arrive in a country, some local people may find it hard to accept them. They may make racist comments or blame the problems in their community on immigrants. People who are racist often refuse to find out what people from other countries and cultures are really like.

Without immigrants, there would not be enough doctors or nurses.

When people are racist, they often make up their minds about people without getting to know them. Local people might say things like, "Immigrants take all our jobs". They have a point of view based on a fixed idea, or "stereotype", of immigrants.

Stereotypes are ways of thinking about an entire group of people. But it is unhelpful and wrong to think that all immigrants are the same. Every immigrant, just like any other member of society, is unique and has different strengths and weaknesses.

Think about it

We can challenge racist stereotypes by showing understanding and awareness. If someone makes rude remarks about immigrants, remind them that many immigrants take on jobs that no one else wants to do, while others have important skills that this country needs. Remember also that everyone has the right to live free from persecution.

"What can I learn from my new classmates?"

It is the differences between people that make life exciting. Our world would be a very dull place without the experience and involvement of people from other cultures. Look around – there are foods, fashions and hobbies from all over the world. Everyone who comes to live in this country can contribute to the community and share the richness of his or her culture.

We can all learn from each other.

If children join your school or move into your street, make an effort to get to know them. Introduce them to rules, routines and activities that they may not be familiar with.

Take the opportunity to learn from them and find out about different ways of life. You may learn new games, taste different foods or simply make new friends.

Did you know...

It's not just people who migrate, food does too! Without people travelling and settling across the world, you might never have tasted some of these items: bananas, beefburgers, chillies, croissants, kiwis, pineapples.

"How can we all live together?"

Racism only divides us and causes problems among communities. It is caused by fear, when people do not understand different cultures.

But with understanding and awareness, both immigrant and local communities can live peacefully alongside each other.

It is important to treat others with respect and understanding.

People will not always agree with others' political views or religious beliefs, but we can respect them.

Be proud of yourself and where you are from. Accept others and remember life is more fun when we enjoy our differences.

My story

"I'm going to Bangladesh to see my aunt and grandma. I really want to show them pictures of my friends here and show them what life is like. My teacher has asked me to keep a diary so I can show my classmates about my trip." Bedana

"What can I do?"

If you have moved to this country:

• Try to join in with as many local activities as possible.

• Be aware that there may be different ways of doing things.

• Tell your classmates and friends about your culture.

• Tell a parent or teacher if you are being bullied.

If someone you know has moved to this country:

• Involve them in activities and make an effort to talk to them.

• Find out about their culture.

• Remember that they may have had terrifying experiences that they may not feel comfortable talking about.

Help new classmates to feel welcome and involved.

Contact information

For further information, contact:

Joint Council for the Welfare
of Immigrants (JCWI)
115 Old Street, London, EC1V 9RT
Tel: 020 7251 8708
www.jcwi.org.uk
Campaigns for justice and combating
racism in immigration law.

United Nations High Commissioner
for Refugees (UNCHR)
Case Posttale 2500, CH-1211
Genéve Dépot, Suisse
Tel: +41 22 739 8111
www.unhcr.ch
Leads and co-ordinates international
action to protect refugees and resolve
refugee problems worldwide.

The Monitoring Group
Emergency helpline: 0800 374 618
Support and assistance for victims of
racial harassment.

Childline:
Tel: 0800 1111
A 24-hour free helpline for children.
www.childline.org.uk

International Organisation for Migration (IOM)
UK: 21 Westminster Palace Gardens
Artillery Row, London, SW1P 1RR
Tel: 0800 783 2332
Australia: P.O. Box 1009
Civic Square, Canberra,
ACT 2608
www.iom.int
Assists in managing
migration and
advancing
understanding of
migration issues.

Racism No Way!
Australia
PO Box 590,
Darlinghurst, NSW 2010
www.racismnoway.com.au
Addresses racism in the
learning environment.

Kids Helpline, Australia
Tel: 1800 55 1800
A 24-hour free helpline for children.
www.kidshelp.com.au

There is lots of useful information about immigration on the internet.

Index

Photocredits

Abbreviations: l-left, r-right, b-bottom, t-top, c-centre, m-middle
Front cover, 8, 26, 27tl – Corel. 1, 6 – Flat Earth. 2, 18, 22 – Brand X Pictures. 3tr – © IOM 2002-MAF0121-Photo: Jeff
Labovitz. 3mr, 7, 23, 24, 29, 30 – Corbis. 3br – Getty Images. 4 – Digital Stock. 5, 9br – Comstock. 9tl – © IOM 2002-MAF0101-
Photo: Jeff Labovitz. 10, 17 – Iconotec. 11 – © IOM 1999-MID0001-Photo: Christopher Lowenstein-Lom. 12 – Anders Nordstrom.
13 - Don Wagner/USCG. 14 – © IOM 2003-MJO0056-Photo: Jean-Phillippe Chauzny. 15, 28 – UNHCR. 16 – Eric Eggen/USCG.
19 – Image 100. 20 – PBD. 21tl – Hollingsworth Studios. 21br - © IOM-HAT0233. 25 – Photodisc. 27br – Ingram Publishing.

To my little friend, Clara Scott-Jones, with love — P.E.

For my wonderful Willow — R.H.

First published in 2005 by Macmillan Children's Books
A division of Macmillan Publishers Limited
20 New Wharf Road, London N1 9RR
Basingstoke and Oxford
Associated companies throughout the world
www.panmacmillan.com

ISBN 0 333 96444 6 (HB)
ISBN 0 333 96445 4 (PB)

1 3 5 7 9 8 6 4 2 (HB)
1 3 5 7 9 8 6 4 2 (PB)

A CIP catalogue record for this book is available from the British Library.

Printed in China by Leo Paper Group

Catch that Kitten!

Pamela Duncan Edwards

illustrated by Rebecca Harry

MACMILLAN CHILDREN'S BOOKS

Tilly has five kittens in her basket.

One,

two,

three,

four . . .

Uh-oh!

Where's Snowball?
Is he in the dolls' house?

No, Snowball is driving the train.
What a **clever** kitten!

Now Tilly has five kittens in her basket.

One,

two,

three,

four...

Uh-oh!

Where's Midnight?
Is Midnight driving the train, too?

No, Midnight is frightening the big dog.
What a **brave** kitten!

Now Tilly has five kittens in her basket.

One,

two,

three,

No, Ginger is playing at dressing-up. What a **funny** kitten!

Now Tilly has five kittens
in her basket.

two,

three,

One,

four... Uh-oh!

Where's Boots?
Is Boots playing at dressing-up, too?

No, Boots is talking on the telephone.

What a **friendly** kitten!

Now Tilly has five kittens
in her basket.

One,

two,

three,

four...

Uh-oh!

Where's Pirate?
Is Pirate talking on the telephone, too?

No, Pirate is hiding in the dolls' house.
What a **silly** kitten!

Now Tilly has five kittens
in her basket.

One, two, three, four . . .

. . . five.

Good night! Sleep tight!

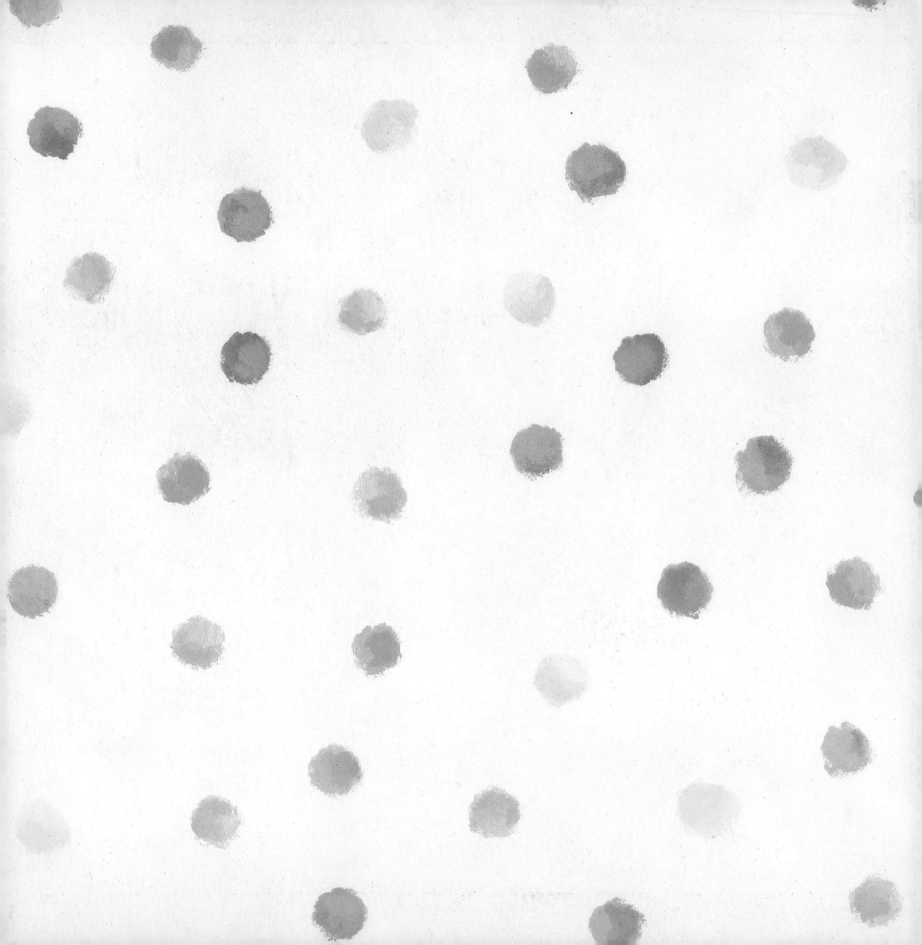